Brandywine Battlefield Park

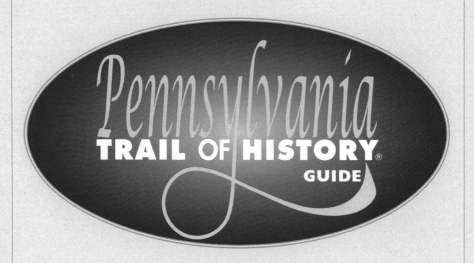

Pennsylvania
TRAIL OF HISTORY
GUIDE

Text by Thomas J. McGuire
Photographs by Craig A. Benner

STACKPOLE BOOKS

PENNSYLVANIA HISTORICAL
AND MUSEUM COMMISSION

Kyle R. Weaver, Series Editor
Tracy Patterson, Designer

Published by
STACKPOLE BOOKS
5067 Ritter Road
Mechanicsburg, Pennsylvania 17055

Pennsylvania Trail of History® is a registered trademark of the Pennsylvania Historical and Museum Commission.

Printed in the United States of America
2 4 6 8 10 9 7 5 3 1
FIRST EDITION

Maps by Caroline Stover

Photography
Craig A. Benner: cover, 3, 5, 12, 15, 16, 18, 19, 21, 22, 30, 31, 36, 39, 42–47

Library of Congress Cataloging-in-Publication Data

McGuire, Thomas J.
    Brandywine Battlefield : Pennsylvania trail of history guide / text by Thomas J. McGuire ; photographs by Craig A. Benner.—1st ed.
        p. cm.—(Pennsylvania trail of history guides)
    Includes bibliographical references.
    ISBN 0–8117–2605–3
    1. Brandywine Battlefield Park (Pa.)—Tours. 2. Brandywine, Battle of, 1777. I. Benner, Craig A. II. Title. III. Pennsylvania trail of history guide.

F159.B73 M38 2001
973.3'33—dc21
                                                                2001020274

Contents

Editor's Preface

As the impetus for their mission to preserve the past, the Pennsylvania Historical and Museum Commission (PHMC) states that they believe "future generations will be strengthened and inspired by the ideals and traditions of Pennsylvania's heritage." This purpose is supported by several visionary objectives, including the goal to "promote partnerships of mutual respect and understanding" with other organizations. Stackpole Books, a publisher in Pennsylvania for more than seventy years, is pleased to work with the PHMC to fulfill this goal with another volume of the Pennsylvania Trail of History Guides, a series of handbooks on the historic sites and museums administered by the PHMC.

The series was conceived and created by Stackpole Books with the cooperation of the PHMC's Division of Publications and Bureau of Historic Sites and Museums. Donna Williams heads the latter, and she and her staff of professionals thoroughly review the manuscripts for historical accuracy and have made many valuable recommendations. Diane Reed, Chief of Publications, has facilitated relations between the PHMC and Stackpole from the project's inception, organized the review process with the commission, and attended to numerous details related to the venture.

For this volume, Connie Stuckert, Administrator of Brandywine Battlefield Park, provided the author and me with access to the site and the appropriate source material for the project's development. The cooperation of her capable staff, including Judy Lupi and Beth Rorke, helped move the project along smoothly. Craig A. Benner, whose images have graced other volumes in this series, has furnished color photographs of battle reenactments, the buildings on the site, and their interiors.

The author of the text, Thomas J. McGuire, is a history teacher, reenactor, and noted authority on the Revolutionary War. He previously wrote about the Philadelphia Campaign in his books *Battle of Paoli* and *The Surprise at Germantown, or Battle of Cliveden, October 4th, 1777*. Here, he offers an overview of events leading to Brandywine, a concise account of the battle, and an armchair tour of the park and its buildings.

Kyle R. Weaver, Editor
Stackpole Books

Introduction to the Site

B randywine Battlefield Park preserves fifty-two acres
of land with historic significance to the Battle of
Brandywine, the devastating Revolutionary War
encounter, in which British forces led by Sir William Howe
defeated George Washington's Continental troops on
September 11, 1777, paving the way for British occupation
of Philadelphia.

Administered by the Pennsylvania Historical and
Museum Commission, the park contains the reconstructed
Benjamin Ring House (Washington's Headquarters), the
original Gideon Gilpin House (Lafayette's Quarters), and
a modern visitor center, which consists of an exhibition
gallery, education center, museum shop, and administrative
offices. The park staff is assisted in its functions by the
Brandywine Battlefield Park Associates, a volunteer support
group.

The Revolution in 1777

L ike the approach of a summer thunderstorm, the rolling peals of cannon fire from the south could be heard all day in Philadelphia. Apprehension gripped the people in North America's largest city, just twenty-five miles from the scene of action, as Gen. George Washington's Continental Army fought to prevent the Crown Forces, commanded by Gen. Sir William Howe, from crossing Brandywine Creek. Rich and poor, black and white, tradesmen and pepper-pot women, congressmen and loyalists alike—all could hear the sound, each with private thoughts about the outcome. On this warm and very humid Thursday, September 11, 1777, the fate of this city, where the Second Continental Congress had met and declared independence just over a year before, hung in the balance.

Brandywine proved to be the largest battle of the American Revolution, as an estimated twenty-six thousand soldiers engaged in desperate combat on the usually peaceful, gentle hills of Chester County, Pennsylvania. The results of the battle determined the course of the Revolution and, ultimately, the fate of the United States of America.

THE WAR BEFORE BRANDYWINE

The American Revolution was into its third year in September 1777 and, like so many wars, had lasted far longer than most people expected. Despite the size and quality of Great Britain's military power, the forces of the United States had managed to survive two and a half years in the field—barely. The previous summer, at the very time when Congress declared independence in Philadelphia, a large British force seized New York City. Washington's Continental Army, at that time numbering about twenty-five thousand (the largest he would ever command), had gathered to defend New York. In the ensuing campaign, Gen. William Howe's army of thirty-two thousand British and Hessian troops, supported by his brother Adm. Richard Lord Howe's fleet, destroyed much of the Continental Army and eventually drove Washington out of New York and into New Jersey.

Exactly one year before the Battle of Brandywine, on September 11, 1776, Adm. Lord Howe met with John Adams, Benjamin Franklin, and Edward Rutledge to discuss a possible end to hostilities. Lord Howe, who was personally

The Nation Makers, 1903. One hundred and twenty-six years after the Battle of Brandywine, illustrator and nearby resident Howard Pyle rendered his memorial to the largest engagement in the Revolutionary War. COLLECTION OF THE BRANDYWINE RIVER MUSEUM (PURCHASED THROUGH A GRANT FROM THE MABEL PEW MYRIN TRUST)

acquainted with Franklin, met the delegates cordially on the western shore of Staten Island, and several hours of talks ensued. In the end, the meeting proved pointless, for nothing less than full British recognition of American independence would end the war. The Staten Island Conference marked the last time that Great Britain spoke to America as colonies.

The New York Campaign continued, and by mid-December 1776 the American cause was near total collapse. The Continental Army was reduced to less than five thousand men and retreated across the Delaware River into Pennsylvania, with remaining enlistments set to expire January 1. Washington wrote that unless some miracle happened, "I think the game will be pretty well up."

Washington's daring Christmas night crossing of the Delaware, leading to the Battle of Trenton on December 26, 1776, and the Battle of Princeton on January 3, 1777, provided the miracle that kept the Revolution alive. The British withdrew their outposts to New Brunswick and Perth Amboy, and Washington spent the next six months at Morristown, New Jersey, harassing their patrols and peppering their outposts with the few troops he had available. All the while, Washington worked diligently to keep up the appearance of strength, while building a new army.

In the spring of 1777, the newly knighted Sir William Howe made what appeared to be preparations for an overland march to Philadelphia. A number of inconclusive maneuvers and skirmishes left officers on both sides puzzled as to Howe's real intentions. In late June, the British evacuated New Brunswick and began moving troops to Staten Island. Washington sent forces down from the ridges behind Bound Brook and Short Hills, only to have

Sir William Howe. Though he sympathized with the American cause at the outset of the war, Howe accepted his orders and arrived in Boston to command the operation at Bunker Hill. He was later named British commander in chief and commenced the 1777 campaign to capture Philadelphia, which climaxed at Brandywine in September. ANNE S. K. BROWN MILITARY COLLECTION, BROWN UNIVERSITY LIBRARY

Howe suddenly turn, divide his army into two columns, and march by night to outflank him. The resulting Battle of Short Hills on June 26, 1777, saw the British successfully turn Washington's left flank. The American army quickly returned to its positions in the hills, while Howe returned to Perth Amboy and proceeded to embark eighteen thousand troops onto ships waiting off Staten Island, their destination: Philadelphia.

THE PROPAGANDA WAR

The people of the Delaware Valley had much to fear from a British invasion, and with good reason. The behavior of the Royal army toward the population of

North Jersey in early 1777 was outrageous. After several instances of assault and rape, Congress convened a special committee to investigate the charges. British and Hessian sources admitted that the indiscriminate plundering of civilians—rebel, loyalist, and neutral alike—was beyond all bounds, especially during the June maneuvers. A young English civilian, Nicholas Cresswell, wrote on June 22: "It is said our Army burnt Brunswick when they left . . . all the Country houses were in flames as far as we could see. The Soldiers are so much enraged they will set them on fire, in spite of all the Officers can do to prevent it. They seem to leave the Jerseys with reluctance."

Reports of this behavior arrived in Chester County via Philadelphia newspapers, soldiers writing home, and travelers passing through. The people were strongly divided over the war, and only a small portion of the population actively supported the fight for independence. Many remained neutral, mainly for religious reasons, or leaned toward support for the British government.

British sources often pointed to the Hessians as the main culprits, Hessian reports carefully noted British-sponsored plundering, and the pro-Revolution newspapers in Philadelphia highlighted the juiciest atrocities. Loyalist papers in New York countered by reporting every instance of plundering by American forces.

The fact was that this propaganda from both sides contained grains of truth. Washington often had his own problems trying to prevent his troops, especially the local militia, from plundering their loyalist neighbors in revenge for British depredations. Concerning the New Jersey militia, Washington wrote to Gov. William Livingston in January 1777:

Their Officers are generally of the lowest Class of People; and, instead of setting a good Example to their Men, are leading them into every Kind of Mischief, one species of which is, Plundering the Inhabitants, under the pretence of their being Tories. A Law should, in my Opinion, be passed, to put a Stop to this kind of lawless Rapine; for, unless there is something done to prevent it, the People will throw themselves, of Choice, into the Hands of the British Troops. But your first object should be a well regulated Militia Law; the People, put under good Officers, would behave in quite another Manner; and not only render real Service as Soldiers, but would protect, instead of distressing, the Inhabitants.

The failure of the British High Command to act quickly and decisively during the spring of 1777 did much more harm than good. By June, when the Crown Forces left New Jersey, they had lost the propaganda war.

MANEUVERS BEFORE BRANDYWINE
The British fleet of 267 ships, commanded by Lord Howe, set sail from Staten Island in late July. Its destination was unknown to the Americans but was presumed to be Philadelphia. In early August, Howe's fleet appeared off the Delaware Bay, prompting Washington to march his army quickly to Philadelphia. But when the fleet again put out to sea in early August, Washington was baffled as to Howe's intentions. After three weeks of waiting, and fearing that Howe's maneuver was simply a trick to keep him away from Gen. John Burgoyne's invasion of upper New York State, Washington ordered the army to march north.

As Washington's army was striking camp, news arrived that the British fleet was in the Chesapeake Bay, heading for northern Maryland. Howe's intentions were now clear: Philadelphia was the target. On August 25, Howe's army began landing at Turkey Point, Maryland, just below Head of Elk, about sixty miles from Philadelphia. Only two natural obstacles remained between the British Army and the capital: the Schuylkill River and Brandywine Creek.

The day before the British landing, Washington's "Grand Army" paraded through Philadelphia, hoping to have an impact "on the minds of the disaffected there." Washington was able to muster about eight thousand regular Continental troops for the parade, and three thousand more were on their way as reinforcements. Additionally, the militias of several local states were called out. Estimates place Washington's forces in early September at twelve thousand regular Continental troops and perhaps three thousand militia. These forces gathered near Wilmington, Delaware, in late August and prepared to block the direct route from the Chesapeake to Philadelphia.

Howe's army spent several days recovering from the voyage, while enduring the humid summer heat and spectacular thunderstorms. Many of the soldiers were seasick after the slow, hot voyage or ill from other causes, especially from consuming spoiled food supplies on shipboard. No sooner had the troops landed than the search for fresh food began, along with plundering. This time, the British commanders acted quickly to control the plundering, but with only marginal success. On August 27, General Howe issued a proclamation reassuring "His Majesty's well-disposed Subjects" that they would be protected if they remained peacefully in their homes. This promise had few believers among the people of the northern Chesapeake, many of whom fled inland.

On the voyage, most of the army's horses had died and were thrown overboard. The remaining animals were in such poor condition that large numbers of them died soon after landing. Howe's army sent out foraging parties to purchase or seize horses, wagons, and livestock. Items not willingly sold to the Royal Army or found on abandoned farms were taken. Those civilians who chose to stay on their farms often were visited again and again by both authorized and unauthorized foragers throughout the campaign. Though many lost their cattle or horses and were subjected to petty thievery, there was no large-scale or indiscriminate burning and looting, as in New Jersey just a few months before.

In early September, the British Army began to move toward Philadelphia. At Iron Hill on September 3, just below Newark, Delaware, British and Hessian light troops encountered the newly formed American Corps of Light Infantry, commanded by Gen. William Maxwell of New Jersey. This special corps, composed of chosen men from the entire army, were blocking the road toward Wilmington at Cooch's Mill. The resulting Battle of Cooch's Bridge, called the Battle of Iron Hill by the British, was a classic light-infantry engagement, small but lively. Casualties on both sides totaled less than one hundred, and the British held the field at the end of the day.

After this small battle, Sir William Howe decided not to march directly toward Washington's army, but instead to use his favorite maneuver: swinging around one of Washington's flanks. Howe's advance forces marched north to Newark, threatening to turn the American right flank and trap the Continental forces against the Delaware River. Washington recognized this possibility and shifted his troops north. Howe continued north to Hockessin Meeting on the main east-west road between Lancaster and Wilmington, and prepared to turn west into Pennsylvania.

George Washington. The Continental commander in chief was painted by Charles Willson Peale in 1776. After the successful New Jersey Campaign, the Virginian would suffer a series of debilitating defeats in Pennsylvania. BROOKLYN MUSEUM OF ART (DICK S. RAMSEY FUND)

On September 9, Washington shifted his army to once more place himself between the British Army and Philadelphia. The Continentals marched northward and westward through hilly country into Chester County to form new positions along a five-mile front on the eastern side of Brandywine Creek, astride the Nottingham Great Road, part of a main north-south route to Philadelphia. Washington took up quarters in the home of Benjamin Ring, a well-to-do Quaker mill owner in Birmingham Township. The American commander had one full day to prepare his position as Howe's army arrived at Kennett Square, about six miles away, on September 10. The stage was now set for the largest battle of the American Revolution.

The Battle of Brandywine

The Continental Army at Brandywine was a newly reconstituted force, painstakingly reassembled after the 1776 New York Campaign. During the winter and spring of 1777, Washington ceaselessly wrote to the states and Congress to send more troops and to regulate the militia that came and went so frequently. The army was reorganized, more regiments were authorized, the enlistment period was lengthened, and new commanders were appointed. But internal tensions became increasingly volatile as some officers received promotions while others found themselves superseded in rank. Issues concerning seniority, pay, and state-related politics fueled discontent throughout the officer corps.

International politics also played a big role in the army of 1777, often to the great frustration of American officers. Numerous French officers and other European professional soldiers arrived, looking for position or adventure in the American service. Many of these officers were promised high ranks by American diplomats in Paris, who were negotiating with the French government for recognition of American independence. Washington referred to "shoals of Frenchmen" arriving in camp during the spring and summer. Some of these officers provided much needed expertise, but others proved troublesome. Thomas Conway and Prud-homme de Borre were French infantry officers who were made brigadier generals in the Continental line. A nineteen-year-old French nobleman with personal connections at court was given the rank of major general by Congress, but no troops to command. Marie Joseph Paul Roche Yves, Gilbert du Motier, Marquis de la Fayette, or, as he is known to most Americans, Lafayette, had his first taste of battle at Brandywine.

The recruitment of regular Continental soldiers proceeded slowly in 1777, especially in Pennsylvania. Washington complained to the Pennsylvania authorities that the state quota was barely one-third filled, and many regiments had only a quarter of their full strength. The reasons for the dismal numbers had to do with internal state politics, political and religious diversity, and unwillingness on the part of many to serve for the

The Continental Army had been reorganized in early 1777, but recruitment was still low.

Marquis de Lafayette. The French noble-man arrived in America three months before Brandywine and immediately won the friendship of Washington, who after the battle wrote that Lafayette "possesses a large share of bravery and military ardor." Charles Willson Peale painted Lafayette around 1781. INDEPENDENCE NATIONAL HISTORICAL PARK

new enlistment period of three years or the duration of the war. The enthusiasm that had reached a peak in the spring and summer of 1776 had dwindled with the news of defeats, stories of the horrors of imprisonment, and the ravages of the greatest killer of soldiers in the eighteenth century, camp disease. Despite these problems, the Continental regulars provided the backbone of American forces, and many showed great skill and bravery at Brandywine.

Militiamen were citizen-soldiers called up for short periods of service, usually sixty days. Failure to respond could result in fines or imprisonment. These troops were often poorly trained, if at all, undependable in battle, and troublesome due to lack of discipline,

especially when dealing with a pacifist local population.

The Crown Forces at Brandywine were made up of regular British Army regiments, Hessian and other German troops hired by the British, and American loyalists. This army was professionally trained, well equipped, and led by professional officers, many of whom were high-ranking European nobility. In addition, it was supplied with hard money, which made the purchase of necessities along the way possible, though very expensive.

Nevertheless, the British had their own problems. Supplying this force was not easy, and uniforms, equipment, and food supplies were not always abundantly available. The long, steamy voyage from New York caused a great deal of spoilage in the food stocks of the Commissary Department. The army made up for it by living off the countryside, much to the annoyance of the inhabitants. Cattle and other livestock were rounded up by the hundreds to feed this army of eighteen thousand troops. Horses were constantly in short supply, and hundreds of wagons had to be procured. The army's tents were left on the ships to shorten the baggage train, so the enlisted men had to either do without shelter or build wigwams, temporary shelters made of brush and other materials. Many of the high-ranking officers brought their personal baggage, and most officers had personal servants.

Discipline and camp security in this army were much tighter than in Washington's army, but unauthorized plundering went on to an alarming degree. General Howe issued a proclamation warning of the severest penalties for plundering, but it was not until a few days after Brandywine that two British soldiers were actually punished by hang-

The British Army was well regulated and disciplined, yet supplying the soldiers in their remote campsites was difficult, leading many to pillage the property of local inhabitants.

ing for the crime. Many of the officers paid lip service to the orders but looked the other way while their men lived off "enemy country."

THE CIVILIAN POPULATION IN 1777

The Battle of Brandywine was fought near the geographic center of Chester County, and the setting for the battle represented the heart and soul of what remained of Quaker Pennsylvania. Though the Quakers were losing political force in Pennsylvania by 1777, the English and Welsh Quaker influence in certain regions surrounding Philadelphia was very strong, especially in the Brandywine Valley. That this area was the scene of the largest battle in the American Revolution was ironic, with the pacifist Quakers dominating the local culture.

In *Letters from an American Farmer*, written in the 1770s, Hector St. John de Crevecoeur asked, "What is an American?" and wrote, "They are a mixture of English, Scotch, Irish, French, Dutch, Germans, and Swedes. From this promiscuous breed, that race now called

Americans have arisen." This description applies perfectly to Chester County. In 1777, the population of the entire county was about twenty-two thousand, the majority of whom lived in the eastern portion, along the Delaware River and its tributaries. (After the Revolution, the county was partitioned, and the city of Chester, the county seat, along with its surrounding townships, became Delaware County.)

Chester County was one of the three original counties established in Pennsylvania by William Penn in 1682, but Europeans had lived within its boundaries since the 1630s, and Native Americans had lived there for centuries before them. The Lenni-Lenape ("the original people") inhabited the region when Penn arrived, but by 1777 their presence was but a memory to the older settlers. The earliest European settlers were Swedes and Finns, who began arriving in the 1630s. Their small numbers had little impact on the area socially in the eighteenth century, but they left one major cultural contribution to the American landscape: the log cabin, hundreds

The Brandywine Valley was predominantly inhabited by English and Welsh Quakers. The Quaker Gideon Gilpin's house was used by Lafayette as quarters during the battle.

bers sought personal communion with God through quiet meditation with the Holy Spirit, or "Inner Light," without ritual, sacraments, or clergy. The Friends emphasized "plainness" in dress and speech, and rejected all forms of violence, especially war.

The Church of England, or Anglican Church, was the state church, headed by the monarch. Those who did not believe in a state-sponsored religion were called nonconformists. The Friends were radical nonconformists who believed that religion should be a matter of personal conscience, not state policy. This viewpoint, at that time considered ultraradical and dangerously subversive, together with the form of Quaker worship—silent meetings—led British authorities to suspect the Friends of being a secret society plotting to subvert Royal authority, and their meetings were prohibited. By the 1670s, many British Quakers began to look for refuge outside the home islands, and the Delaware Valley beckoned as new territory. When, in 1681, King Charles II suggested that land west of the Delaware River could be used to pay a debt he owed Adm. Sir William Penn (d. 1670), William Jr. saw a great opportunity to establish a "Holy Experiment."

Quakers in England and Wales responded enthusiastically to the new colony, and the Brandywine Valley drew English Quakers, such as the Ring and Gilpin families, together with Welsh Quakers, including the Jones and Davis families. Within a short period of time, Friends meetinghouses, plain buildings often first built of log and later of stone or brick, marked the beginnings of

of which dotted the Brandywine Valley. The Dutch, who initially claimed the area, lost their North American empire to the English in the 1660s, but Dutch settlers continued to migrate to the Delaware Valley in small but steady numbers well into the eighteenth century. The name Brandywine probably derives from Andren Brainwinde, a Dutch settler who came to the region about 1670.

British settlers began arriving in the 1670s, even before William Penn was granted the land. Penn and other Quaker leaders had been interested in establishing a Quaker refuge in America for several years due to persecution. Religion and politics were intertwined in seventeenth-century Britain, resulting in serious religious strife and civil war. It was during this period that the Society of Friends, or Quakers, appeared as a nonviolent Christian sect whose mem-

small, tight-knit communities, together with mills, blacksmith shops, and taverns. Local artisans soon began to produce well-made furniture, pottery, and extraordinary clocks.

In the following years, large numbers of English settlers moved to Chester County, along with Welsh and, to a lesser extent, Germans and Swiss (whom the English called "Dutch"), and a few French Huguenots. Many of the "Dutch" were Anabaptists—Mennonites and Amish—who espoused nonviolence, as did the Quakers. Small numbers of Africans were brought to Pennsylvania in the seventeenth century as slaves. At first, some British Quakers had no qualms about slave ownership, but by 1777, few Quakers were slave owners; many more Friends became active in antislavery movements. Most Africans in eighteenth-century Pennsylvania, slave or free, lived in Philadelphia. The number of slaves in Chester County was never large, and by 1782, county records indicate that out of about three hundred servants, white and black, in the whole county, one hundred were slaves, or less than one-half of 1 percent of the county population.

Some parts of Chester County, and many of the frontier areas of Pennsylvania, were settled in the mid-eighteenth century by Scots-Irish Presbyterians from Ulster in Northern Ireland. These fractious, combative Ulstermen had limited tolerance for pacifist Quakers, even less for Germans, and very little at all for Indians. As these new waves of settlers pushed beyond the Susquehanna River into the Blue Mountains, the French and Indian War forged a new breed of Pennsylvanian, one very different from Penn's vision: the frontiersman. The political scene in Pennsylvania shifted from Quaker control in the 1750s and became more fragmented and con-

tentious, as non-Quakers demanded a greater say in the provincial legislature. When Parliament attempted to stop further westward expansion and settle conflicts with the Indians by issuing the Proclamation of 1763, seeds of resentment against the British government, planted long before in Ulster, began to blossom into resistance.

By 1775, nurtured by events in New England, the resistance ultimately bloomed into Revolution in parts of Pennsylvania. The Brandywine Valley, however, remained largely English Quaker in culture and appearance: quiet, prosperous, plain, and industrious. A few Friends decided to take an active stand for or against independence, but those who in any way actively supported the war effort were "read out" of their meetings. Most Quakers remained neutral and unsupportive of the war, or spoke against war and resistance to the government, while continuing their private concerns. In the apprehensive and unsettled situation of 1777, as events beyond their control brought war to their doorsteps, this course of action earned them the contempt of the Revolutionaries, who labeled them as traitors, Tories, or subversives. The adjutant general of the Continental Army, Timothy Pickering of Massachusetts, wrote to his brother on September 25, 1777, two weeks after Brandywine:

I feel in some degree reconciled to Howe's entering Pennsylvania and Philadelphia, that the unworthy inhabitants (of which 'tis apparent a majority of the State is composed) may experience the calamities of war, which nothing but their own supineness and unfriendliness to the American cause would have brought on them. Possibly Heaven permits it in vengeance for their defection, that their country should be the seat of war.

The Barns and Outbuildings near the Gilpin House at Brandywine Battlefield Park exhibit the plain and functional Quaker architecture that was typical of the Brandywine Valley in 1777.

THE BRANDYWINE VALLEY IN 1777

If ever there was a vision of an eighteenth-century peaceable kingdom, it was in the Brandywine Valley. Few places on earth have been blessed with such a variety of excellent natural resources. The countryside is pleasing to the eye, with lush, green, rolling hills, large stands of hardwood trees, and countless natural springs of sweet water. The soil is some of the richest in the world and provides well-watered land for raising grain and superb livestock.

Excellent building materials were among the local resources: tawny limestone; gray mica schist, or "glimmer stone"; great, round, melon-size stones of black basalt; brown ironstone; creamy white quartz; and a peculiar green stone called serpentine. In addition, clay deposits supplied material for bricks. Iron ore was plentiful, and burnt limestone provided lime for mortar and fertilizer. The countryside was dotted with solid houses and barns, workshops, taverns, and places of worship. The architecture and locally made furniture reflected the ethnic background of the population, with an overriding Quaker emphasis on plainness, simplicity, and usefulness. The Brandywine and its tributaries provided waterpower for sawmills, gristmills, fulling mills, oil mills, and ironworks.

It is not surprising that so many English and Welsh settlers made the area their home, for the countryside closely resembles parts of England and Wales. During the Battle of Brandywine, a British officer remarked to a local boy, "You have got a hell of a fine country here, which we have found to be the case ever since we landed." An old tradition holds that another British officer had a premonition of his own death when he reached Osborne's Hill near Birmingham Meeting House, for "the scenery before him was as familiar to him as the scenery of his native place in Northumberland." The predominantly English flavor of the area carried over into such local township names as Birmingham, Kennett, Marlborough, Bradford, and Thornbury.

The Brandywine itself gave definition to the area. Above Chadds Ford, it is referred to as a creek; below the ford, it is called a river. In the days before the battle, several rainstorms had raised the water level significantly. The Brandywine occupies a large floodplain of dramatically varying widths and depths and is often quite deceptive, for the floodplain contains marshes, small islands, and swampy bottoms. About six miles northwest of Chadds Ford is the Forks, where the waterway divides into the eastern and western branches and continues for many miles to its headwaters in upper Chester County.

Crossing the Brandywine safely in the eighteenth century meant finding a ford, a place where the bottom was solid enough and the water shallow enough to allow horses and wagons to cross. There were also a few ferry crossings, where a large wooden raft carried traffic, guided by a rope slung between the banks and pulled by a ferryman. The fords and ferries were given the names of local eighteenth-century property owners: Pyle, Gibson, Chads, Brinton, Wistar, Jones, Buffington, Jeffries, Taylor, and Trimble. All of these crossings played a role in the Battle of Brandywine.

From a military perspective, the landscape presented a variety of problems and opportunities for both armies. The rolling hills and wandering creeks were perfect for defense, if properly manned and held. Most of the open fields were fenced by strong, four or five-rail wooden fences, called railings. Thick stands of trees provided cover for light troops and infantry in open formation. The irregular nature of the ground allowed forces moving on the offensive to use the terrain to screen their movements, provided they had knowledge of the area.

One of the most basic elements in any successful military operation is having good information about the terrain and the roads. In the summer of 1777, the commanders of both armies had to rely on the knowledge of local people, as no detailed maps of the Brandywine region were available to them. One of the few benefits of the passage of the armies through the area was the production of several maps, showing the natural terrain as well as roads and important buildings.

WASHINGTON'S POSITION

On September 10, Washington placed his troops along the eastern side of Brandywine Creek, straddling the main road north to Chester and Philadelphia. This road crossed the Brandywine at Chads' Ford (now Chadds Ford). The Continentals began to construct earthen batteries for the artillery just north of the ford, behind the Chads house, to cover the ford and provide support for the center of Washington's line.

Washington's left flank was held by nearly two thousand Pennsylvania militia, commanded by Gen. John Armstrong, on hills several hundred yards south of the main road, covering Gibson's Ford and Pyle's Ford. Chads' Ferry,

Washington's Forces at Brandywine numbered approximately 13,000 and consisted of Continental regulars from Pennsylvania, New Jersey, Maryland, Virginia, Delaware, and North Carolina, as well as militia from Pennsylvania.

a crossing about five hundred yards south of Chads' Ford, was guarded by Gen. Nathanael Greene's Division of eighteen hundred Virginia Continentals. The ford itself, on Greene's right, was defended by Gen. Anthony Wayne's Division of Pennsylvania Continentals, about sixteen hundred strong. These two divisions formed the center of Washington's position.

A mile north of Chads' Ford was Brinton's Ford, held by twelve hundred Maryland Continentals under Gen. John Sullivan. Another mile or so farther up on the right flank was Jones' Ford, guarded by eighty soldiers of the Delaware Regiment, while two hundred troops of the 1st Battalion of Hazen's Regiment covered Wistar's Ford, another mile to the right. The next ford up, Buffington's, just below the Forks of the Brandywine, was covered by Hazen's 2nd Battalion of two hundred men and marked the extreme right flank of the line.

American intelligence sources mistakenly reported that due to high water, the next feasible crossing place above Buffington's was Taylor's Ferry, twelve miles above Chads' Ford, and too far for an army to reach from Kennett Square and return to Chads' in one day. The mistake proved to be critical: The next ford up, Jeffries', was only eight miles above Chads'. The roads to it from Kennett Square were convoluted, however, and the ford was deep, so it was left unguarded.

The remainder of the Continental Army—forty-three hundred strong—remained behind Greene and Wayne, providing defense in depth at the center of Washington's line, where the main attack was expected. Finally, Washington sent a corps of eight hundred men, composed of Maxwell's Light Infantry Corps, some Continental Light Dragoons, and

companies of Chester County militia, across Brandywine Creek at Chads' Ford to act as the advance guard and to give plenty of warning of the British approach. These troops patrolled the area west of the Brandywine toward Kennett Square.

THE BRITISH STRATEGY

By the time of the Battle of Brandywine, Sir William Howe had been commander in chief of British forces in North America for over two years. His first battle in the Revolution had much to do with his overall strategy. At Bunker (Breed's) Hill in 1775, he led his favorite troops, the British Light Infantry, in an attempt to turn the American left flank on a narrow beach. His "light bobs" were stopped dead in their tracks by concentrated musket fire at close range from Americans secured behind hastily built fortifications. All twelve officers on Howe's personal staff were killed or wounded. Howe was unhurt, but he was covered with blood at the end of the day. Since that day, after witnessing scores of light infantrymen drop in heaps on that bloody beach, Howe's general strategy had been to avoid head-on frontal assaults against fixed positions. Instead, he would try to lure American forces out into the open and then send troops around the flanks, forcing his opponents to shift their positions, retreat, or face being surrounded.

The largest land battle in the war to date had been the Battle of Long Island, fought in late August 1776. There, Howe had used this flanking strategy and all but annihilated the Continental forces in Brooklyn, inflicting nearly fifteen hundred casualties, while suffering less than four hundred of his own. But then, much to everyone's surprise and to the great annoyance of many of his officers,

Howe's Army at Brandywine consisted of about 15,000 men, including British regulars, Hessians, and loyalists.

Howe did not press his advantage. He chose not to renew the assault the following day, effectively allowing Washington's army to escape. This pattern was repeated more than once, and Brandywine was no exception.

On the evening of September 10, the Crown Forces were encamped at Kennett Square, about six miles southwest of Chads' Ford. Some local loyalists, including the high sheriff of Chester County, came to Howe's headquarters and offered their services as guides. The British Army's chief spymaster was Pennsylvania's most famous loyalist, Joseph Galloway, a wealthy Philadelphia lawyer and former speaker of the Pennsylvania Assembly. Galloway organized the local guides and introduced them to General Howe. They informed Howe of exactly where Washington had placed his army along Brandywine Creek, naming fording places, roads, and hills, and then told the British commander ways he could get around Washington's lines, pointing to the unguarded fords above the Forks: Trimble's Ford on the western branch and Jeffries' Ford on the eastern branch, only two miles above Buffington's. By

midnight, Howe's strategy of sidestepping Washington's army had turned into confrontation, on Howe's terms.

The British Army was made up of two divisions. Lord Cornwallis commanded the main division, made up of Howe's best troops: two British Guards Battalions, the 1st and 2nd British Grenadier Battalions, three Hessian grenadier battalions, the 1st and 2nd British Light Infantry Battalions, the Hessian Jäger Corps (riflemen, also called chasseurs), the 3rd British Brigade, and the 4th British Brigade. This force numbered about eight thousand men, supported by artillery.

The other division, commanded by a Hessian officer, Lt. Gen. Wilhelm von Knyphausen, was made up of the 1st British Brigade and 2nd British Brigade, a Hessian brigade of four regiments, two battalions of the 71st Highland Regiment, and light troops composed of American loyalists and British riflemen. This made a total of nearly seven thousand troops, plus artillery. The rest of the force acted as reserves or guarded the baggage train, which stretched for several miles behind Knyphausen's column.

TACTICS

Brandywine was a classic eighteenth-century battle fought in the European manner, with modifications to suit conditions in America. The popular images of clever Colonial marksmen wisely taking cover and mowing down line after line of bumbling, overdressed, red-coated automatons in tight formations are part of Revolutionary folklore but have no basis in fact at Brandywine.

The bulk of the Continental Army stood in linear formations in the open or under cover of trees, as the terrain permitted, and the British and Hessians were well served by their light troops, who fought using "ranger" or light infantry tactics. The regular British infantry stood in open formation—that is, troops were spaced at arm's length in line rather than shoulder-to-shoulder. British troops threw themselves flat on the ground from time to time to take cover from American volleys, which may partially account for the discrepancies between American accounts about massive, sustained gunfire and large numbers of British casualties seen from the Continental positions, and the relatively small number of actual casualties.

Joseph Townsend remarked after the battle near Birmingham Meeting, "We hastened thither, and awful was the scene,—to behold such a number of fellow-beings lying near each other, severely injured, and some of them mortally; a few dead, but a small proportion, considering the quantity of powder and balls that had been used."

The troops on both sides generally followed the prescribed rules of linear warfare established by military experts in Europe. These rules were dictated by three important factors: the weapons technology of the eighteenth century; the mechanical problems associated with moving large bodies of soldiers from place to place to keep them organized for effective maneuvering against their opponents and win the battle; and the social systems of European and American society, which dictated who led and who followed.

On their way into Pennsylvania, these two divisions often marched by different roads, heading in the same direction whenever possible, to move the army quickly over a large area and for security. Knyphausen arrived at Kennett Square first, and his division occupied the main road heading east toward Chads' Ford. Cornwallis arrived by way of a crossroad on Knyphausen's right, and his troops marched straight through Kennett Square, heading north toward Marlborough Township. Thus the British camp at Kennett Square was cross shaped, as both columns stretched a few miles on either side of town, with Cornwallis's column heading north, perpendicular to Knyphausen's column heading east.

After receiving detailed information from the local guides about the position of Washington's forces, Howe decided to once more exercise his strategy of outflanking his opponent. Knyphausen's column would be sent toward the American front at Chads' Ford, with instructions to "amuse" the Americans: fire artillery, make as many troop movements as possible, and give Washington the impression that the main attack would be there. Cornwallis's column would move north through hilly countryside west of the Brandywine, using the hills and woods as a screen, and cross the creek above Washington's right flank. Once this force was across, it would move east and south to strike the right of Washington's army or, if possible, move behind the Continentals and attack from the flank and the rear.

THE BATTLE: PHASE I

At first light, about 5 A.M. on September 11, Cornwallis's division moved out from Kennett Square and headed north. The day began with typical late-summer weather for the region: early-morning fog and haze, which gradually burned off by midmorning, resulting in a muggy, humid day that turned uncomfortably warm by midafternoon. British movements were partially screened by the fog in the morning, though in the early afternoon the march of Cornwallis's column was confirmed by a large cloud of dust spotted by American scouts.

Knyphausen's column, which left Kennett Square about 8 A.M., made the first contact with Washington's forces at Welch's Tavern, about halfway between Kennett Square and Chads' Ford. Horsemen from Baylor's Continental Light Dragoons encountered the Queen's Rangers, an American loyalist regiment commanded by Capt. James Wemys, together with Ferguson's Rifle Corps, British sharpshooters equipped with a new breech-loading rifle invented by the unit's commander, Capt. Patrick Ferguson. Both of these advance British units were dressed in green uniforms.

The Continental dragoons fell back from Welch's Tavern toward Kennett Meeting House, just over a mile away. As the Rangers pursued the dragoons, a company of Continental light infantry fired on the loyalists from a concealed position and then withdrew. Another hidden company also fired and fell back, drawing the Rangers even closer to Kennett Meeting. The bulk of the Continental light infantry took up positions near the meetinghouse, and some were posted behind the meetinghouse wall. They put up a stubborn fight and inflicted significant casualties on the Queen's Rangers. But the action here was only meant to delay the British advance, and Maxwell slowly withdrew back down to Chads' Ford.

The Kennett Friends Monthly Meeting was scheduled for that day, and as the Quakers chose to ignore war and all of its preparations, the meeting was

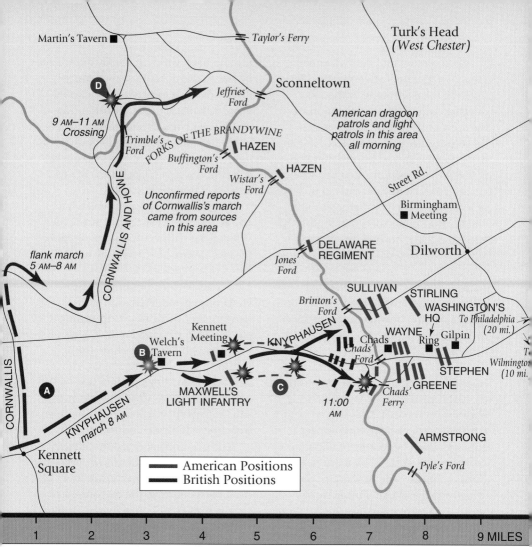

Phase I, 5:00 A.M.–11:00 A.M. **A** *British routes of march.* **B** *First encounter, 8:00.* **C** *Stubborn skirmishing toward Chads' Ford.* **D** *Probable scene of 11:00 skirmish.*

held. Hannah Pierce, a Quaker woman confined to her home by illness, wrote: "This day was a very trying time. The English army was marching through the neighborhood, and as it was the usual time for Kennett Monthly Meeting, it was difficult for Friends to get there." Her brother-in-law, Jacob Pierce, reported that at the meeting, "While there was much noise and confusion without, all was quiet and peaceful within."

A series of small, sharp actions occurred on the hilly, broken ground between Kennett Meeting and the ford. At one point, the Queen's Rangers advanced toward some American troops who appeared to be surrendering, only to be fired upon suddenly at close range; dozens of Rangers fell in this ambush.

Ferguson's Corps also suffered heavily, losing nearly two-thirds of its strength by the end of the battle, while

Ferguson was severely wounded and lost the use of his right arm.

As Knyphausen's column pushed the Continentals down into the valley at Chads' Ford and Chads' Ferry, his artillery began to deploy on the heights west of the creek. British and Hessian infantry moved south of the ford toward the ferry and north of the main road toward Brinton's Ford, about one mile north of Chads'. By midmorning, Maxwell's Light Infantry had fallen back across the Brandywine, and a lively but ineffective artillery barrage across the creek began about 11 A.M., continuing for the next few hours. The valley between the two armies shook and reverberated with the thunder of cannons from both sides, and the humid air quickly filled with clouds of thick, white smoke. Knyphausen was following his instructions to "amuse" the Americans and patiently waited to hear gunfire from the north, which would indicate that Cornwallis had gained Washington's right flank.

Cornwallis's Flanking March

As Knyphausen engaged the advance corps of Washington's army, Cornwallis's column moved north. This main British column marched over narrow roads through well-screened countryside toward Trimble's Ford on the west branch of the Brandywine, about two miles above the Forks. The column was nearly five miles long, and moving at an uneven rate of about two miles per hour. Reaching Trimble's Ford about 9 A.M., the column crossed the creek and halted to rest and dry off.

In the midmorning hours, probably just after resuming the march at Trimble's Ford, the rear of this column was fired on by a patrol of Pennsylvania riflemen, and a sharp skirmish ensued. The Americans withdrew, and their com-

mander, Lt. Col. James Ross of Lancaster, a regular officer of the Pennsylvania Line, sent a message to Washington: "Great Valley Road Eleven O'Clock A. M. Dear General, A large body of the enemy from every account 5000, with 16 or 18 field pieces, marched along this road just now." Ross went on to describe where the road could possibly lead the British: farther north to Taylor's Ford and to the Ship Tavern on the Lancaster Road in the Great Valley, or east to Jeffries' Ford and Dilworth's Tavern. The report also mentioned that Joseph Galloway was with this column, as was General Howe, and that Galloway had spoken to many of the neighborhood people. Several local inhabitants, including one Curtis Lewis, a landowner in West Bradford (the township into which Cornwallis's column had just entered), acted as guides under Galloway's direction.

Washington received this message about noon. It confirmed an earlier report sent from Gen. John Sullivan that Col. Moses Hazen, who was stationed at Jones' Ford, had learned that the British were definitely making the flank movement. Ross's information was the third report Washington had received that morning concerning the British flank march. But the first report had been unconfirmed, and Maj. John Jamison of Bland's Dragoons had reported from the right flank at 9 A.M. that there was no enemy activity there. This message was incorrectly interpreted to mean that the British weren't making the march. They were, in fact, on the march, but had not yet arrived in the area where Jamison was patrolling and would not arrive there until midafternoon.

In response to Ross's report, Washington decided to launch an attack on Knyphausen. He ordered Sullivan to cross the Brandywine at Brinton's Ford and directed Maxwell to take his light

Charles, Lord Cornwallis *commanded the main division of British troops at Brandywine.* LIBRARY OF CONGRESS

infantry back across at Chads' Ford. Maxwell moved out quickly, drove back some of Knyphausen's advance pickets, and overran a British artillery battery that was under construction. Sullivan's advance forces, intending to turn Knyphausen's left flank, crossed at Brinton's Ford and skirmished with the British 4th Regiment.

This was the crucial moment in the Battle of Brandywine. Had Washington launched a full-scale attack against Knyphausen, he might have been able to defeat the Crown Forces at Chads' Ford, changing the outcome of the battle significantly. But at this critical moment, General Sullivan received another report that Cornwallis's column was nowhere to be seen west of the Brandywine or near the Forks. This report came from Maj. Joseph Spear of the 8th Chester County Militia, a local officer who knew the area well. Sullivan wrote Spear's information down and sent it to Washington immediately:

Since I sent you the message [earlier] . . . I saw Major Spear of the militia who came [last night was crossed out and changed to] this morning from a Tavern called Martins in the Forks of the Brandywine. He came from thence to Welches Tavern and heard nothing of the Enemy [being] about the Forks of the Brandywine & is confident that they are not in that Quarter. So Hazen's information must be wrong.

Martin's Tavern was located only a mile and a half north of Trimble's Ford in present-day Marshallton, at the junction of "the Great Valley Road" (now Northbrook Road), the "road to Taylor's ferry" (Strasburg Road east from Marshallton), and the road "to the Great Valley at the Sign of the Ship" (Strasburg Road west and the Marshallton-Thorndale Road). In other words, Spear's route from Martin's to Welch's tavern took him down the very road that Cornwallis's column moved up. The important question here is, just when did Spear travel over the road? The message had the words "last night" crossed out and changed to "this morning." But what time that morning? The changed wording of the message suggests that it was so early in the morning that Spear passed along the road *before* Cornwallis's column moved over it.

This report caused Washington to hesitate and rethink his strategy. The American commander evidently believed that Cornwallis's march was a feint to get Continental troops across the Brandywine so he could then reverse his march and hit them from the flank and the rear. Washington recalled Sullivan back across the creek and sent more scouts out to gather intelligence. He was also becoming irritated that he had not heard from his own chief intelligence gatherer, Col. Theodorick Bland, of Bland's Light Dragoons, who was scouting the roads somewhere above Jones'

THE STORY OF SQUIRE CHEYNEY

The main source for the story of Thomas Cheyney's attempt to warn Washington of the whereabouts of approaching British troops is Sarah Frazer, the daughter of Col. Persifor Frazer. She recounted the story in 1840. At the time of the Battle of Brandywine, she was only eight years old. Despite these facts, the rest of her narrative about her father at the battle is considered accurate by historians. Her narrative of the Cheyney episode, as recorded in *General Persifor Frazer, A Memoir* (Philadelphia, 1907), follows.

Thomas Cheyney Esquire, a good staunch whig, but withal a plain, blunt country farmer, when he heard the firing that morning, threw his saddle on his lightfoot hackney mare and rode off towards Birmingham without dressing himself at all; had neither coat nor stockings on—he knew the country well and rode about the hills until he saw the main body of the enemy marching up the west-side of the river, *when he rode full speed to where General Washington was stationed and told him. He also informed him that they could not cross until they had passed the forks in which time Washington could have a party up; two hundred he said would be sufficient to stop them in the narrow defile they must pass in coming down this side. The General did not seem to give much credence to the information as his Aides had been out and had given no such word, moreover he could not tell whether Cheyney was friend or foe, as his appearance was the same as the great body of tories in the country. The dear old Whig's feelings were wrought up to a great pitch, so that he fairly trembled with agitation when he said, "If Anthony Wayne or Pers. Frazer were here you would know whether to believe me or not," and as he thought the people about the General seemed to look rather sneeringly at him he clenched his hand and said, "I have this days work as much at heart as e'er a Blood of you."*

Ford. Col. Timothy Pickering, the adjutant general of the Continental Army, noted that about noon, Washington "bitterly lamented that Col. Bland had not sent him any information at all, and that the accounts he had received from others were of a very contradictory nature." Several hours went by with no word from the right flank.

THE BATTLE: PHASE II

In the meantime, Cornwallis's men continued their march by turning east and heading for Jeffries' Ford, about two miles from Trimble's. Between 12 noon and 2 P.M., this column crossed the east branch of the Brandywine and headed up the road toward Birmingham Meeting House. At the head of the column were the German riflemen called Jägers (the British and Americans called them chasseurs; both words mean "hunter"). The advance guard was led by Captain Johann Ewald, accompanied by a few British light infantrymen and a company of Scottish Highlanders. Ewald cautiously moved through a very steep defile from Jeffries' Ford up to Sconneltown, a crossroads hamlet about half a mile east of the ford. The defile was wedged between two high hills, and Ewald expected an ambush at any moment. Reaching the top, he was astonished to discover that the Americans were "half an hour away" (about two miles, for light troops), near Birmingham Meeting House. He noted that a hundred men posted at the defile could have held up the army all day.

At the top of these hills, just past the defile, was a large wheelwright shop in Sconneltown (and little else), occupied

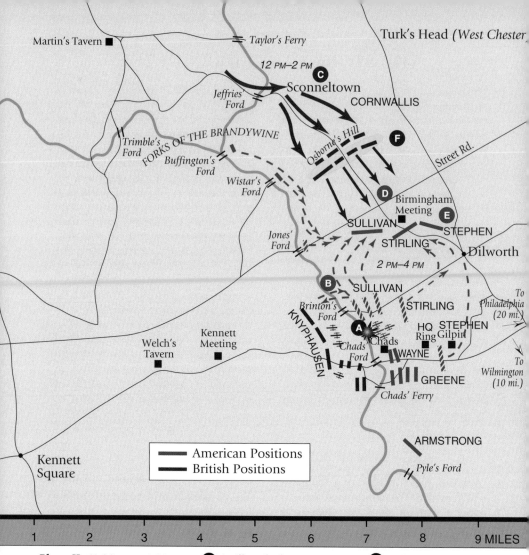

Phase II, 11:00 A.M.–4:00 P.M. **A** *Artillery duel, 12:00 to 2:00.* **B** *Sullivan crosses Brinton's Ford, then is recalled and sent to Birmingham.* **C** *Joseph Townsend and Friends encounter Cornwallis's column.* **D** *Bland spots Cornwallis's column at 1:30.* **E** *Stirling and Stephen converge near Birmingham, then meet Sullivan and redeploy.* **F** *Cornwallis's assault, 4:00.*

by Quakers from Birmingham Meeting. Their meetinghouse had been taken over by the Continental Army for use as a hospital, so the Birmingham Friends decided to hold their Fifth Day, or mid-week meeting, in Sconneltown.

During the meeting, a disturbance was heard outside, and some of the Friends went out to see what was going on. Joseph Townsend, a Quaker teenager

who was present, said that the meeting concluded when the commotion increased and those who went outside did not return. The commotion turned out to be caused by some local women who were in a panic, hearing that the British Army was coming and fearing that they would all be murdered. As some of the Friends tried to calm their fears, Townsend noted:

Our eyes were caught on a sudden by the appearance of the army coming out of the woods into the fields belonging to Emmor Jeffries, on the west side of the creek, above the fording-place. In a few minutes the fields were literally covered over with them, and they were hastening towards us. Their arms and bayonets, being raised, shone as bright as silver, the sky being clear and the day exceedingly warm.

This sight had quite an impact on the local residents. For many, the largest gathering of people they had ever witnessed was at church or meeting, or perhaps a public event at a local tavern. Those who went into Philadelphia for market days might have seen a few thousand people on Market Street, but most had never seen more than a few hundred gathered at one time. Further, the Quakers of late-eighteenth-century Pennsylvania dressed in plain clothing, often of drab gray or brown, and the men usually wore broad-brimmed hats. Here, coming across the creek, was a grand spectacle of military pomp, color, and glittering pageantry, the very antithesis of the Brandywine Valley Friends.

The force crossing at Jeffries' Ford was led by Hessian Jägers dressed in uniforms of green with red facings and brass buttons, accompanied by Scottish Highlanders in jackets of red and blue, dark tartan kilts, red and white argyle stockings, and blue bonnets ornamented with checkered headbands and black plumes. Behind them came hundreds of grenadiers, men noted for their height and physical size. There were eleven hundred British grenadiers in red coats, thirteen hundred Hessian grenadiers in blue uniforms, and thousands of other British regulars and light troops. Interspersed along the line were dragoons and artillery pieces. Even with a coating of dust from the march, the troops were dazzling.

Mindful of the reports and rumors from North Jersey earlier that year, Joseph Townsend and his brother William headed for home, fearing that it might become a target for plunder, or worse. Townsend's parents were away, and his sisters were the only ones home. After a short while, with no troops approaching the Townsend house, the two young Quaker brothers could not resist viewing the scene and went back to the main road. Here they found the army heading up the road toward Birmingham Meeting House. Joseph noted that the column of troops and the flankers on both sides of the road covered a front about half a mile wide.

The Townsend boys and other civilians went in among the troops and were treated cordially. Soldiers and officers alike asked them where the rebel army was, and Joseph and William were asked by some high-ranking officers "where *Mr. Washington* was to be found." William told them to have patience and they would meet him in a short time. When asked what sort of man Washington was, William, who had seen the American commander at Chads' Ford the day before, said "he was a stately, well-proportioned, fine-looking man of great abilities, active, firm, and resolute, of a social disposition, and was considered to be a good man." One of the British officers testily replied, "He might be a good man, but he was most damnably misled to take up arms against his sovereign."

At Richard Strode's house, about a mile south of Sconneltown, Joseph Townsend saw Lord Cornwallis: "He was on horseback, appeared very tall and sat very erect. His rich scarlet clothing, loaded with gold lace, epaulets, etc., occasioned him to make a fine martial appearance." Later in the day, Townsend also saw General Howe: "He was mounted on a large English horse, much

THE WEAPONS

The weapons technology of the eighteenth century involved several types of firearms, all of which played an important part at Brandywine. The main weapon used by all the forces involved was the firelock, a smoothbore, muzzle-loading flintlock musket. These weapons fired a large-caliber round, lead ball with a maximum effective range up to about 150 yards, but due to the weapon's inaccuracy, firing was often done at much closer ranges and in volleys. The weapons could be loaded and fired effectively two or three times per minute on average by a well-trained soldier. The general idea was to have large bodies of troops form in two-rank lines, move close to their opponent, and fire by sections, with both ranks firing together, to fill the air with masses of musket balls. The volume of firepower compensated for the lack of accuracy in the individual weapons.

One of the most important features of the military musket was the bayonet, a blade that fit onto the end of the musket barrel, essentially turning it into a spear. It was the most effective edged weapon carried by a foot soldier. In the British Army, bayonets were typically eighteen inches long and were triangular at the base, tapering into a sharp point. A bayonet charge could carry the day, as well-led troops advancing en masse with fixed bayonets presented a frightening spectacle that instilled panic in their opponents. Bayonet charges were effective in sweeping the enemy right off the field, often with no physical contact between the forces. This sort of maneuvering required skill and discipline on the part of the soldiers for maximum effectiveness. It also required competent leadership from officers, whose personal appearance and behavior in battle had a direct effect on the morale and performance of the soldiers in the heat of the firing.

British troops mostly carried the 2nd Model Long Land Pattern "Brown Bess" musket, a .75-caliber weapon that fired a .69-caliber round, lead ball. Hessian troops usually carried German-made muskets of various types and different large calibers. Continental troops were armed with an eclectic assortment of whatever was available, though one British officer noted that most of the muskets dropped by retreating American troops were .69-caliber French Charleville muskets.

reduced in flesh (from the long voyage). . . . The general was a large, portly man, of coarse features. He appeared to have lost his teeth, as his mouth was somewhat fallen in." About the British commanders overall, Townsend observed that "most or all of the officers who conversed with us were of first rank, and were rather stout, portly men, well dressed and of genteel appearance, and did not look as if they had ever been exposed to any hardship; their skins were as white and delicate as is customary for females brought up in large cities or towns."

As the British forces approached Osborne's Hill, the troops stopped to rest and eat their dinner. A small contin-

In addition to the smoothbore military musket, both sides had small forces of riflemen. The rifle had spiral grooves, or rifling, cut into the inside of the barrel. The bullet fit tightly in the barrel so that when the weapon was fired, the spiral grooves gave the bullet a spin as it left the barrel, thus increasing the bullet's range and accuracy. Rifle fire could be deadly up to about three hundred yards, depending on the powder, the wind, the weapon, and the marksman's skill.

The rifle had two disadvantages when compared to smoothbore military muskets: Because the bullet fit tightly into the barrel, it was slow to load—about a minute to a minute and a half per shot—and it was not designed to carry a bayonet, which gave the musket the advantage at close range. Gen. Anthony Wayne stated flat-out, "I don't like rifles," saying that a soldier properly uniformed and equipped with a musket and bayonet was a much more formidable opponent in battle.

The British Army did employ riflemen, who functioned together with British light infantry. In early 1777, Ferguson's Corps of English Riflemen was formed and equipped with a new weapon, the Ferguson rifle. This firearm was a breechloader, loaded from the back, or breech, rather than a muzzleloader, loaded from the

front, or muzzle. It was a short, carbine-style firearm that could be loaded and fired up to six times per minute—twice the rate of the smoothbore musket—and it was rifled, giving it great accuracy at two hundred yards.

The Pennsylvania rifle of the Revolution has entered into the realm of legend, and Pennsylvania riflemen were present at Brandywine, though the most famous group of them, Morgan's Rifle Corps, were with the northern army under General Gates in upstate New York.

The artillery played a big role in the Battle of Brandywine. Washington's army was equipped with about sixty fieldpieces, ranging in size from three-pounders to six-pounders (so named for the weight of the cannonballs they fired). The British and Hessian forces had close to ninety guns, ranging from medium twelve-pounders to light three-pounders. These cannons were capable of firing solid shot, exploding shells, or grapeshot, small iron balls in clusters that were effective against massed infantry. The artillery duels at Brandywine, especially across Brandywine Creek at Chads' Ford, were some of the more spectacular features of the battle.

gent of Hessian Jägers and Scottish Highlanders under Captain Ewald was sent forward to scout the area near Birmingham Meeting House. Walking up the north side of Osborne's Hill, Joseph Townsend, along with a companion, "proceeded through the crowd on the public road until we reached the advanced guards, who were of the German troops. Many of them wore their beards on their upper lips, which was a novelty in that part of the country."

Cornwallis's Position Spotted
About a mile farther up the road, Col. Theodorick Bland of the Continental Light Dragoons hastily scribbled a message to Washington: "1/4 past one

o'clock. Sir, I have discovered a party of the Enemy on the Heights just on the right of the Widow Davis's who live close together on the road call'd Forks road, about half a mile to the Right of the Meeting House. There is a higher hill on their front." Bland also sent a message to Sullivan at Brinton's Ford, who notified Washington: "Dear General, Colo. Bland has this moment sent me word, that the enemy are in the Rear of my Right, about two miles, coming down, as he says, about two Brigades Chasseurs [Jägers]. He also says he saw Dust Rise back in the country for about an hour. . . . 2 o'clock p. m."

Upon receiving this information, Washington ordered two of his reserve divisions, Stirling's and Stephen's, to march quickly toward Birmingham Meeting House. These divisions totaled about thirty-five hundred men from Virginia, Pennsylvania, and New Jersey. Each division took a different route and had to march between four and six miles over hilly terrain. At 2:30, Sullivan received orders to march to Birmingham with his division of about thirteen hundred Marylanders and to take command of all the forces on the Continental right flank.

Stirling's and Stephen's troops began arriving near Birmingham Meeting House at about 3 P.M. and took up positions on a hill south of the building. Sullivan's troops began arriving shortly thereafter, approaching from the west, and taking positions on a hill about half a mile to the left, in front of Stirling's men.

THE BATTLE: PHASE III
At 4 P.M., having rested and eaten, Cornwallis's troops prepared for battle. They dropped their packs and blankets in great heaps and formed into three columns on Osborne's Hill. On the left flank, east of the Forks Road, from left to the center, were the 1st and 2nd British Light Infantry battalions and the Hessian Jägers, a total of about sixteen hundred men. In the center, on the road in column, supporting the advance, came thirteen hundred Hessian grenadiers, followed by the 4th Brigade, with the 3rd Brigade in reserve. On the right flank, in the position of honor, were the 2nd and 1st British Grenadier Battalions, eleven hundred strong, with nine hundred men of the two British Guards Battalions on the far right.

Now came a show of military pageantry so spectacular that those who witnessed it never forgot it. On the march, the British grenadiers had worn small cloth foraging caps, reserving their elegant bearskin caps for battle or for formal occasions. Colonel Meadows, commander of the 1st Grenadier Battalion, roused his troops with the cry: "Grenadiers, put on your caps! For damn'd fighting and drinking I'll match you against the world!" The grenadiers took the regulation fifteen-inch-tall bearskin caps out of their knapsacks (the bearskins were designed to pack flat), brushed them up, and put them on. The silver and black cap plates glittered with the king's arms and the motto *Nec Aspera Terrent*—"Hardship does not deter us"— as the companies formed into columns of battalions. With battalion flags unfurled and the musicians playing "The Grenadiers March," the crimson lines steadily advanced down the south front of Osborne's Hill in a front stretched out for over half a mile. One British officer wrote, "Nothing could be more dreadfully pleasing than the line moving on to the attack; the Grenadiers put on their caps and struck up their march, believe me, I would not exchange those three minutes of rapture to avoid ten thousand times the danger!" Joseph Townsend, who had walked up the road toward

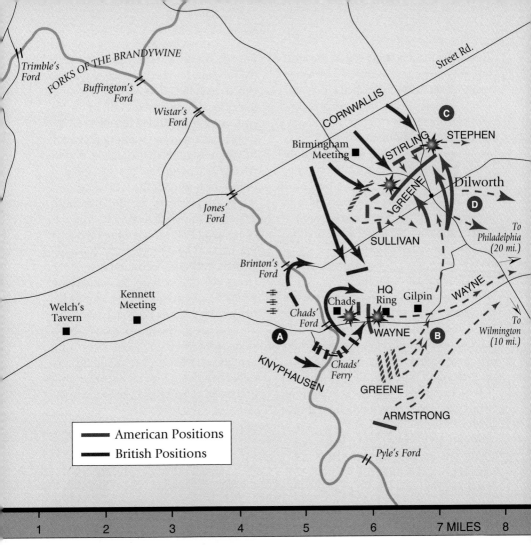

Phase III, 4:00 P.M.–8:00 P.M. (A) *Knyphausen begins cannonade and assault, 5:00.*
(B) *Greene rushes to Sandy Hollow to reinforce right wing.* (C) *See-saw battle at Sandy Hollow; Lafayette wounded.* (D) *Retreat to Chester, 8:00.*

Birmingham Meeting with a friend, noted, "On turning our faces back we had a grand view of the British army, as they advanced over and down the side of Osborne's Hill and the lands of James Carter, scarcely a vacant space left."

Fully taken with the awesome sight, Townsend and his companion momentarily forgot that deadly combat was about to transpire. "While we were amusing ourselves with the wonderful curiosity before us, to our great astonish-

ment and surprise the firing of musketry took place." The Hessian Jägers in the advance guard were fired on by some Americans in an orchard about two hundred yards in front of Birmingham Meeting House. This was Capt. Thomas Marshall's 3rd Virginia Regiment, posted in advance of the American position. The Jägers and the British advance parties took cover along the embankment at Street Road, returned fire, and waited for the main force to arrive. Joseph

Townsend moved to get out of the area, but not before he was ordered by a German officer, "who flourished a drawn sword over my head," to remove fence rails to allow some companies to form up in the fields along the road. While doing so, young Joseph realized that this could be construed as actively assisting in the demise of his fellow beings, which ran contrary to the pacifist principles of the Friends. In the ensuing confusion, Townsend was able to get away, and he returned to Osborne's Hill.

General Sullivan's Blunder

The British and Hessian advance parties had noticed considerable movement in the American lines. From his position on Osborne's Hill, General Howe could see large bodies of Americans filing off to their right. What the advance parties saw were Stirling's and Stephen's troops, who had arrived on a hill behind Birmingham Meeting House, shifting their position to the right. About half a mile to the left and in front was a large hill, later known as Battle Hill, where Sullivan's Division was heading. Once Sullivan's troops arrived on the hill, Sullivan rode over to consult with Stirling and Stephen, and they agreed that Stephen's troops would shift their position to the right and change their front so that Sullivan's men could come into line on the left and close the half-mile gap between them. What Howe probably saw from Osborne's Hill was Sullivan's troops filing off to the rear to perform the maneuver.

While this confused and untimely maneuvering was taking place, the British main attack, advancing under heavy artillery fire, struck the left of the Continental Army's right wing. Near Street Road, Cornwallis halted his advance and had the men deploy from columns into battle lines. The British

Guards, on the extreme right of Cornwallis's line, had become separated from the British grenadiers, so the Hessian grenadiers maneuvered to fill in the gap. As Cornwallis resumed the advance, Sullivan's division was caught unprepared in the midst of its maneuvering, and the left of the Continental line collapsed under the assault of the Hessian grenadiers. In the chaos, the 2nd Maryland Brigade, commanded by Gen. Prudhomme de Borre, mistakenly fired into the 1st Maryland Brigade, and a panic ensued, effectively eliminating the Maryland Division. Stirling's Jerseymen and Pennsylvania troops in the center held firm at first but were driven back by the onslaught. The British grenadiers charged bayonets and rushed the Continentals, who fell back through the area called Sandy Hollow. Lt. Ebenezer Elmer of the 3rd New Jersey Regiment wrote:

John Sullivan. *The major general from New Hampshire led a division of Maryland Continentals at Brandywine and unwittingly maneuvered them into disaster.*

We Came in Sight of the Enemy who had Crossed the river & were coming down upon us; we formed ab[out] 4 oClock on an Eminence, the right being in ye woods, presently a large Column Came on in front playing ye Granediers March & Now the Battle began wh[ich] proved Excessive severe[. T]he Enemy Came on with fury[;] our men stood firing upon them most amazingly, killing almost all before them for near an hour till they got within 6 rod [33 yards] of each other, when a Column of the Enemy came upon our flank wh[ich] Caused them to give way wh[ich] soon extended all along ye line; we retreated & formed on ye first ground and gave [them] another fire & so continued on all ye way, but unfortunately for want of a proper Retreat 3 or 4 of our [artillery] pieces were left on ye first ground.

East of the Forks Road, the British Light Infantry and Hessian Jägers attacked Marshall's troops, who had taken positions behind the stone wall of the Birmingham Meeting Yard, and, after stubborn resistance on the part of the Continentals, drove them back. The Royal light troops now hit Stephen's Division, posted on a "ploughed hill" on the right of Sullivan's line, and forced them to withdraw a few hundred yards to a ridge behind Sandy Hollow. A see-saw battle ensued as troops re-formed, charged bayonets, and furiously rushed each other. In the midst of this fighting, nineteen-year-old Marquis de Lafayette attempted to help rally some of Conway's troops in Stirling's Division. At one point, his aide pointed out that blood was pouring out the top of his boot; Lafayette had been shot clean through the calf. He was taken from the field and bandaged and was eventually sent to a hospital in Bethlehem, Pennsylvania.

This was the scene of some of the most intense combat in the American Revolution. In places, the fighting became hand-to-hand; the firing was

AFRICAN AMERICANS AT BRANDYWINE

Americans of African descent played important roles in America's fight for independence. By 1777, whites and African Americans served side-by-side in the Continental Army. At Brandywine, the Army was composed of soldiers from regiments mostly raised in the middle and southern states, along with volunteers from a number of European nations. In some of the regiments from the middle states, free African Americans also served in the ranks as musketmen and musicians, while others provided important support services as teamsters and laborers. For example, Edward "Ned" Hector was a teamster attached to Hercules Courtney's battery of Proctor's Pennsylvania artillery, stationed at Chads' Ford. As British forces surrounded the battery, the gunners were ordered to abandon their cannons and wagons and retreat. Hector refused to leave his ammunition wagon and was credited with saving not only the ammunition but also weapons dropped by retreating soldiers. For his services in the Revolution, Hector received a pension of $40 from the state of Pennsylvania.

close and furious, and one officer noted that the common distance between the lines was about forty yards. Numerous officers on both sides later wrote that they had never heard such sustained gunfire as in this phase of the Battle of Brandywine. Artillery and musket fire thundered across the landscape in one continuous roar, and the air filled with dense, choking clouds of acrid, white gunpowder smoke, which hung in the humid air, reducing visibility to near zero. Col. James Chambers of the 1st Pennsylvania Regiment, stationed at Chads' Ford, wrote that "the cannonade [on the right wing] commenced about three o'clock, but soon gave way to small

RELIVING THE REVOLUTION

The photographs of battle reenactments in this book were taken at the Brandywine Battlefield Park during Rev Times, an annual event that brings the battle to life for the public. Reenactors in authentic period clothing demonstrate soldier life, weapons, tactics, camp activities, and a large-scale battle. Contact the site for more information on the event and on the other programs held throughout the year (see page 47).

arms, which continued like an incessant clap of thunder, till within an hour of sunset, when our people filed off." The sound traveled as far as twenty-five miles away; the people of Philadelphia could clearly hear the cannon fire, and from the outskirts of the city, vollies of musketry could be distinguished in the distance.

From Chads' Ford, Washington wrote to President John Hancock in Philadelphia at 5 P.M.: "At half after four O'Clock, the Enemy attacked Genl Sullivan at the Ford next above this and the Action has been very violent ever since. It still continues. A very severe Cannonade has begun here too and I suppose we shall have a very hot Evening. I hope it will be a happy one." When he was informed that Sullivan's force had been pushed away from Birmingham Meeting, Washington ordered Gen. Nathanael Greene's Division, made up of Weedon's and Muhlenberg's Brigades, to

move away from Chads' Ferry and march to the right wing on the double. Weedon's troops set something of a record, reportedly moving four and a half miles in forty minutes. These troops arrived near the crossroads village of Dilworth at about 6 P.M., in time to reinforce Sullivan's troops, which had fallen back about a mile south of Birmingham Meeting. Washington, with part of his staff, also headed toward the right to try to reorganize the confused situation.

Across Brandywine Creek, General von Knyphausen could also hear the battle at Birmingham. At 4 P.M., Knyphausen formed his men for the attack across Chads' Ford. British and Hessian artillery opened fire at 5 P.M. on Wayne's Division, and Proctor's Continental Artillery returned fire from the hill behind the Chads House. British and Hessian troops advanced toward the ford and toward Chads' Ferry, a few hundred yards downstream. The British and Hessian artillery fire ceased, and British troops, led by the 71st Highlanders, entered the creek up to their waists. American artillery sprayed the crossing with grapeshot, and the Brandywine ran red with British blood. Still the troops pressed onward, securing the left bank at Chads' Ferry. Other British and Hessian forces crossed and fanned out to the left, moving up along the creek toward Chads' Ford and Brinton's Ford, passing below the range of the batteries on the heights above them.

Maxwell's Light Infantry held the Chester Road (now Route 1), supported by Wayne's Division. To the far left, below the ferry and out of supporting range, was the Pennsylvania militia under Gen. John Armstrong. British light troops began skirmishing with Maxwell in the Chester Road, while other British forces climbed the hills and surrounded Proctor's artillery. As more and more of Knyphausen's column filed across the creek, Wayne's troops took up positions in the vicinity of the Ring House. Colonel Chambers described it:

The troops that were on the right of our brigade, on the hill, were drawn off. . . . The enemy kept an unremitting fire from their artillery (and ours too played with great fury), until advancing under the thick smoke they took possession of the redoubt in front. . . . Our men were forced to fly, and to leave three [artillery] pieces behind. Our brigade was drawn into line . . . and my right was exposed. The enemy advanced on the hill . . . and came within fifty yards of the hill above me. I then ordered my men to fire. Two or three rounds made the lads clear the ground. . . . The main body of the foe came within thirty yards, and kept up the most terrible fire I suppose ever heard in America. . . . We retreated to the next height in good order, in the midst of a very heavy fire of cannon and small arms.

Nathanael Greene of Rhode Island commanded a division of Virginia Continentals that marched to reinforce Sullivan's badly beaten Marylanders in the twilight of the battle. Charles Willson Peale painted Greene's portrait in 1783. INDEPENDENCE NATIONAL HISTORICAL PARK

Stubborn hill-to-hill fighting ensued, but the British had gained the high ground to the right of the Chester Road. As darkness fell, elements of the British Guards Battalions, which had been on the extreme right of Cornwallis's division, began to appear on Wayne's right, threatening his line of retreat and forcing the Continentals to withdraw toward Chester.

The fighting continued until dark, with both sides rushing reinforcements to the area around Dilworth. As darkness fell and the sounds of battle at Chads' Ford indicated a successful British assault there, Washington ordered a general retreat toward Chester. The battle near Dilworth ended with a small but dashing cavalry charge led by a Polish volunteer officer, Count Casimir Pulaski. This charge helped to discourage further British advances on the retreating Continentals.

THE AFTERMATH

Brandywine was the largest and longest battle of the American Revolution. Maneuvers commenced before dawn; firing began just after sunup and, with a few pauses during the course of the day, lasted until after dark. The exact casualties for both sides will never be known with any certainty, as each side tended to maximize their opponent's casualties and minimize their own. Estimates for both sides run as high as 2,000, but most likely, Washington lost about 300 killed, 600 wounded, and 300 captured. The official British casualty report admits a total of 543, including 90 killed, about 400 wounded, and many missing. This number is almost certainly an underestimate, based on the descriptions of fighting in various parts of the field, especially near Dilworth.

Washington's army retreated to Chester that night and toward Philadelphia the next day. General Howe requested American surgeons to work with the Continental Army wounded, as he had no surgeons to spare. Local buildings, including Birmingham Meeting House, were turned into hospitals for the wounded. Joseph Townsend, who walked over the battlefield after the fighting ended, was pressed into service by the British surgeons to assist the wounded. He saw the doors torn off the meetinghouse and converted into operating tables. Joseph witnessed an amputation, which took about twenty minutes, without anesthetics or antiseptics. Not surprisingly, as soon as darkness and confusion permitted it, he escaped and headed home.

The Battle of Brandywine was a strategic and tactical masterpiece for Sir William Howe. Everything he had planned to do in the battle succeeded brilliantly, and he forced Washington's army into headlong retreat toward Chester and Philadelphia. Howe's chief flaw was his failure to follow up his advantage and destroy the Continental Army, much to the frustration of many of his officers. Had he done this, it might have brought the war to an end with a British victory. This failure to pursue Washington after the battle allowed the Continentals not only to survive, but to recover and remain an effective fighting force.

Washington's generalship in this battle, by contrast, was marked by apparent indecisiveness and hesitancy, traits that often plagued him throughout the war and that frustrated many of his officers. Col. Timothy Pickering wrote that this was Washington's major flaw as a com-

Anthony Wayne held his Pennsylvania Line at Chads' Ford throughout most of the battle, until heavy firing in the last phase finally forced his retreat to Chester. His portrait from the late 1790s is attributed to Sharples. INDEPENDENCE NATIONAL HISTORICAL PARK

The Defeat at Brandywine was, for the Continentals, the low point of the Revolution. If Howe had taken advantage of the situation, he could have crushed Washington and brought an end to the rebellion.

mander, and nowhere was it more evident than at Brandywine. Although faulty and contradictory intelligence was the main factor in Washington's hesitancy, his overcaution cost him the battle. Had Washington followed his own initial instincts, which were based on repeated previous experiences with Howe, Brandywine might have been a spectacular American victory, and Howe's own cautions might have been his undoing.

Fifteen days after Brandywine, on the morning of September 26, 1777, Lord Cornwallis entered Philadelphia with the British and Hessian grenadiers to settle in for a nine-month occupation of the rebel capital. On October 4, Washington would go on the offensive and strike Howe's army at Germantown, hoping to drive him from the city. Failing in this attempt, the Continental Army waited for another opportunity to strike the Crown Forces, only to have the onset of winter change their plans. On December 19, 1777, the campaign for Philadelphia ended and Washington's

army began a new kind of battle—a battle against the elements—at Valley Forge.

THE BATTLEFIELD

The British Army left the Brandywine area early on the morning of September 16, 1777. The dead who were found after the battle were buried in parcels near where they fell; many of the graves were left unmarked and have since disappeared. The local residents worked for years to restore their farms to their prewar condition, and many chose to forget the traumatic events of September 11. Quaker principles forbade the commemoration or memorialization of such events, except perhaps as a verbal reminder of why war is to be avoided.

Over the years, visitors came to the area to view the battlefield, including the Marquis de Chastellux and other French officers with the Rochambeau expedition to Yorktown in 1781. The first significant postwar attention paid to Brandywine occurred when the Marquis de Lafayette returned on his American tour in 1824. Lafayette was greeted with

OTHER SITES OF INTEREST

The Brandywine Battlefield is a National Historic Landmark and was the first site in Pennsylvania to be named a Commonwealth Treasure, in 1997. Most of the battlefield remains in private hands, and unfortunately, some of it has not been preserved. Efforts are under way to save those significant portions that are currently threatened with private development. Other existing sites significant to the battle but not operated by the Brandywine Battlefield Park are listed below.

① JOHN CHADS HOUSE

The John Chads House, built in the 1720s, still stands in Chadds Ford. Elizabeth Chads occupied the house during the battle and refused to leave, fearing that it would be plundered. Proctor's Continental artillery occupied the hill behind the house and was the center of Washington's defenses at Chads' Ford. The house is beautifully restored and maintained by the Chadds Ford Historical Society. The building is located on PA Route 100 just a few yards north of U.S. Route 1 in Chadds Ford.

② BARNS-BRINTON HOUSE

This brick dwelling was built in 1714. It had operated as a tavern in the early part of the century, but was the Brinton family residence at the time of the battle. Though the house played no direct role in the battle, skirmishing raged in its vicinity all morning on September 11, and General Knyphausen's troops marched past the old landmark. The building is well preserved and maintained by the Chadds Ford Historical Society as a fine example of a Colonial tavern. The Barns-Brinton House is located on the south side of U.S. Route 1 about one mile west of Chadds Ford.

③ KENNETT MEETING AND
④ BIRMINGHAM MEETING

These two Quaker meetinghouses are both well-maintained eighteenth-century structures, and their character has not changed in two centuries. Birmingham is still in active use by the Friends, and visitors are welcome. In the adjoining burial yards are graves of soldiers who died in the Battle of Brandywine. One grave at Kennett is marked "ye Hessians," and a large stone marks a mass grave at Birmingham Meeting. Please be respectful of these places of worship. Kennett Meeting is located on the north side of U.S. Route 1, about three miles west of Chadds Ford. Birmingham Meeting is on the east side of Birmingham Road, between PA Route 926 and Dilworthtown.

bands and military delegations, and he toured the battlefield. It was at this time that he pointed out the general area of the field where he was wounded. He also visited the elderly Gideon Gilpin, who had hosted him before the battle and was now near death.

Just after the Civil War, a few private markers inscribed with poetry relating to Lafayette and the battle were placed in the cemetery adjoining Birmingham Meeting. At the Centennial of 1877, some cannons were placed to mark the scene of the fighting near Sandy Hollow, one of which alleges to point out the spot where Lafayette was wounded.

Later, in 1893, a monument was erected along Birmingham Road by the schoolchildren of Chester County to commemorate the wounding of Lafayette.

In the early 1900s, sixteen bronze tablets were placed by the Commonwealth of Pennsylvania at various spots to guide visitors through the area; eight of these markers remain today. The land, however, remained privately owned, much of it by the same families who had held it in the eighteenth century. The largely Quaker population in the area generally continued to ignore the battle and its commemorations, as had their ancestors.

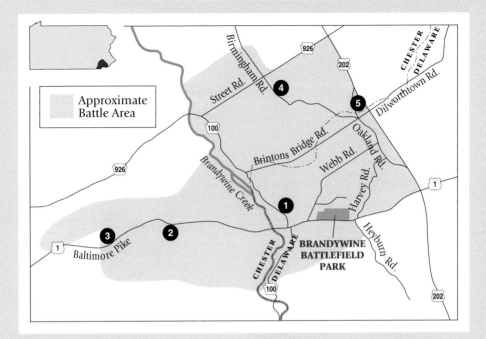

5 DILWORTHTOWN AND THE DILWORTHTOWN INN

The village of Dilworthtown still maintains its eighteenth-century character, with several stone houses, a store, a forge, and a tavern. The brick tavern, the Dilworthtown Inn, dates from 1758 and was considerably plundered by the British after the battle. The battle ended in this vicinity as night fell, and Washington's forces retreated east toward Chester. British and Hessian forces occupied the ground here for the next five days. The Dilworthtown Inn is located at Old Wilmington Pike and Birmingham Road, about a quarter mile west of U.S. Route 202.

With the development of railroads, trolley lines, and the automobile, Americans in the early twentieth century began to travel as never before, and many people visited historic sites on Sunday outings. State and local governments responded to the demand for historic preservation by private citizens and to the general trend fostered by President Theodore Roosevelt's land conservation efforts, and historic sites in many areas became the focus of preservation.

In 1947, the Commonwealth of Pennsylvania established a park to commemorate the Battle of Brandywine. Though its boundaries include only a fraction of the battle area, the park contains the original house that Lafayette made his quarters, as well as a reconstruction of the house that served as Washington's headquarters. The park is today the primary destination for information on the Battle of Brandywine, as its staff has been in the forefront of the continuing effort to preserve the rest of the battlefield. It is the mission of the park to commemorate and interpret the battle for the public.

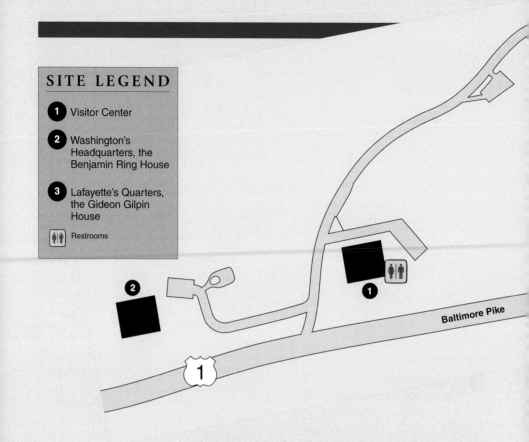

SITE LEGEND

1 Visitor Center

2 Washington's Headquarters, the Benjamin Ring House

3 Lafayette's Quarters, the Gideon Gilpin House

👫 Restrooms

Baltimore Pike

1 (US Route 1 marker)

---

1 **VISITOR CENTER**

The Visitor Center houses a permanent exhibit, containing artifacts, maps, and information about the Battle of Brandywine. Visitors can see a bronze cannon identified by General Lafayette in 1824 as one of the guns dragged away from the battle, an original 1768-pattern British grenadier's bearskin cap, cannonballs and other battle relics, and a working replica of the rare Ferguson rifle, a British-made breech-loading weapon first used in major combat at Brandywine. An eighteen-minute video documentary about the Battle of Brandywine brings the largest battle of the American Revolu-

tion to life, using reenactors to depict the course of the battle and explore its impact on the area and the local people, as well as its aftermath. The education center provides space for school groups and contains many visual aids of soldiers, uniforms, maps, and artifacts.

Hands-on materials include reproduced clothing and equipment for students to see and hold. The museum shop has an extensive collection of reading materials and other products relating to the American Revolution and Colonial life.

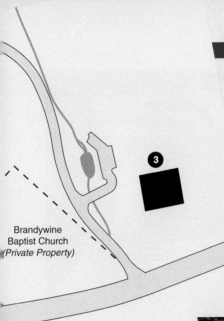

Brandywine
Baptist Church
(Private Property)

Visiting the Park

② WASHINGTON'S HEADQUARTERS, THE BENJAMIN RING HOUSE

The Ring House is a reconstruction of a southeastern
Pennsylvania center hall stone
Colonial house. A fire in the
1930s destroyed the original
house. The exterior of the
reconstruction is accurate and
was based on photographs
that were taken before the fire.
Some rooms in the interior
were also rebuilt from photo-
graphic documentation—the
kitchen, for instance—but others were based on conjecture.
The plan suggests to the visitor
the appearance of the building
as it might have looked when
General Washington occupied
it in September 1777. The
building's general appearance
both inside and out is evoca-
tive of the houses in the neighborhood.

Some information does exist about the owner of the property and his family. In September 1777, Benjamin Ring was a prosperous and well-respected local businessman. He owned a gristmill and a fulling mill (used for cloth processing and dyeing) and was a sawmill operator. The Rings also owned 160 acres in the area. Benjamin was forty-eight years old; his wife, Rachael, was thirty-eight years old and four months into her ninth pregnancy. The couple had been married nineteen years and had seven living children, ranging in age from one to seventeen. Chances are that there was a sick child in the house, for eight-year-old Lydia died in October 1777. Although they were Quakers, Benjamin and his eldest son Elias were listed in the Chester County militia.

Washington's army arrived in the area on September 9, and it is probable that Washington spent two nights with the Ring family. The general had his military family with him: up to nine aides-de-camp, nine servants and household staff, plus numerous officers and messengers visiting, consulting, and constantly moving in and out. The house would have been very crowded, cluttered, and smoky; this might explain the confusion concerning exactly where Lafayette stayed. It is quite possible that he stayed with Washington in the Ring House for one night and moved to the less chaotic Gilpin House for his second night.

3 LAFAYETTE'S QUARTERS, THE GIDEON GILPIN HOUSE

The Gilpin House was used by General Lafayette as his quarters before the Battle of Brandywine. The main part of the house was built of local stone in about 1745. It is technically described as a tradesman's house or Penn Plan house, meaning that the floor plan follows the plan proposed by William Penn for workmen's dwellings. A smaller section on the east side of the dwelling follows a much older pattern but was added later, suggesting that it was dismantled and moved to the site from elsewhere. This section follows a very old-fashioned English construction of beams infilled with bricks, or "noggins," and is sheathed on the outside with clapboard.

At the time of the battle, thirty-eight-year-old Gideon Gilpin and his thirty-four-year-old wife, Sarah, lived here with their six children (four boys, two girls), all under the age of fourteen. The average Chester County farm in 1777 was about 120 acres; the Gilpin farm was larger, consisting of 193 acres, 130 of them improved and 63 uncultivated. The Gilpins were Quakers, though Gideon appears in the muster lists of Col. John Hannum's Battalion of Chester County militia. Aside from this, the Gilpins were a typical Brandywine Valley family, with a good house, good land, and a good-size family. After the battle, Gideon Gilpin put in a claim for damages done to his property by the British Army, in the amount of 502 pounds, 6 shillings Pennsylvania currency.

Little is known about Lafayette's stay here. He was a few days shy of his twentieth birthday and had been with the Continental Army for only a few weeks. For political reasons, due to his connections in the French court, Congress had made Lafayette a major general, but he had no troops under his command. Some period accounts suggest that he stayed at the Ring House,

which served as Washington's headquarters. But when Lafayette returned to visit Brandywine Battlefield on July 26, 1825, "about a mile from the ford [Chads' Ford] the general stopped and alighted from his carriage to see Gideon Gilpin, a very aged man, confined to bed, at whose house he had made his headquarters before the battle." Gideon would have been eighty-six years old at this time. "The sick man was gratified at the sight of the veteran, who pressed his hand cordially and wished him every blessing."

The Gilpin family furnishings are gone; in their place is furniture typical of that found in a prosperous Chester County yeoman farmer's or tradesman's house of the period, as listed in wills and house inventories in the county records. The furniture is of local make and design and is sturdy, plain, and well used.

For information on hours, tours, programs, and activities at Brandywine Battlefield Park, visit **www.ushistory.org/brandywine** or call **610-459-3342**.

Further Reading

Boatner, Mark M., III. *Encyclopedia of the American Revolution.* 3rd ed. Mechanicsburg, Pa. Stackpole Books, 1994.

Commager, Henry Steele, and Richard B. Morris, eds. *The Spirit of Seventy-Six: The Story of the American Revolution As Told by Participants.* 1958; reprint, New York: Bobbs-Merrill Company, 1976.

Cummings, William, and Hugh Rankin. *The Fate of a Nation: The American Revolution through Contemporary Eyes.* London: Phaidon Press, 1975.

Dann, John C., ed. *The Revolution Remembered: Eyewitness Accounts of the War for Independence.* Chicago: University of Chicago Press, 1980.

Fleming, Thomas. *Liberty!: The American Revolution.* New York: Viking Books, 1997.

Futhey, J. Smith, and Gilbert Cope. *The History of Chester County.* Philadelphia: Louis Everts, 1881. Source of Townsend quotations.

Gifford, Frank. *The American Revolution in the Delaware Valley.* Philadelphia: Pennsylvania Society of Sons of the Revolution, 1976.

Reed, John Ford. *Campaign to Valley Forge, July 1, 1777–December 19, 1777.* 1969; reprint, Philadelphia: University of Pennsylvania Press, 1990.

Smith, Samuel Stelle. *The Battle of Brandywine.* Monmouth Beach, N.J. Philip Freneau Press, 1976.

Trussell, John B. B. *The Pennsylvania Line: Regimental Organization and Operations, 1775–1783.* Harrisburg, Pa.: Pennsylvania Historical and Museum Commission, 1977.

Weslager, C. A. *Dutch Explorers, Traders, and Settlers in the Delaware Valley, 1609–1664.* Philadelphia: University of Pennsylvania Press, 1961.

Wright, Esmond, ed. *The Fire of Liberty.* New York: St. Martin's Press, 1983.